D1228435

ROBERT BARCLAY

Photo. J. D. Yeadon, Elgin.

GORDONSTOUN HOUSE.

ROBERT BARCLAY

HIS LIFE AND WORK

BY

M. CHRISTABEL CADBURY

HEADLEY BROTHERS
BISHOPSGATE, LONDON, E.C.
1912

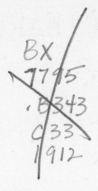

HEADLEY BROTHERS,
PRINTERS,
LONDON AND ASHFORD, KENT.

CONTENTS

LIST OF ILLUSTRATIONS

ROBERT BARCLAY

CHAPTER I

INTRODUCTION

AMONG the many religious sects which came into being during the seventeenth century, the Society of Friends was one of the most conspicuous. Its founder, George Fox, the son of an obscure weaver, taught that God speaks directly to every man, and guides all who are willing to be guided. His followers were commonly called Quakers,[1] because he bade men tremble at the word of God.

[1] " Justice Bennet, of Derby, was the first that called us Quakers, because I bade them [the Justices] tremble at the word of the Lord."—George Fox *Journal*.

Thousands gathered to hear his preaching, and through it found inward peace which before they had sought in vain. By degrees they came to realize that this was the peace which Christ had promised to His followers. They set before themselves therefore the aim of being "Christians in good earnest"; they protested against everything which they considered contrary to Christ's teaching, and they tried to live their lives in accordance with His law of love. All other religionists agreed that the Quakers were a "damnable sect . . deluded by Satan," though in the practical affairs of life, even their adversaries admitted that they were, for the most part, a clean and upright people. The followers of Fox belonged mostly to the labouring and artisan class. Like Fox himself, they were men of little or no education in the ordinary sense of the word. But there were notable exceptions, and among

Nicol, contemporary diarist.

these was Robert Barclay, who was an aristocrat and a scholar. He set himself to prove that though the followers of Fox might be, for the most part, ignorant and illiterate men, yet their beliefs were in accordance with " scripture, reason, and true learning." The work with which his name will always be connected is entitled " An Apology for the True Christian Divinity, as the same is held forth and preached by the people called, in scorn, Quakers." But he also wrote many other works in support of Quakerism. George Fox wrote to him on one occasion :

" And now, Robert, concerning the things thou speaks of about thy books, I say it is well that they are sent. Keep within the rules of the spirit of Life, which will lead into all truth. . . So all that have the in-strument to work in God's vineyard be not idle, but be diligent that you may have your penny."

Barclay used his "instrument" to great purpose. His writings raised the controversy which was raging around Quakerism from the level of ignorant abuse, and established it upon a basis of intelligent criticism and enquiry. Among his contemporaries, his most famous opponent was John Norris, an Anglican philosopher and divine, who, in replying to the "Apology," pays this tribute to its author :—

"Two Treatises concerning the Divine Light," by John Norris, M.A., 1692, Part II, pp. 1 and 32:

"Mr. Barclay is a very great man . . . I know of no Church . . . but might well be proud of the accession of so considerable a writer; the general contempt they lie under does not hinder me from thinking the Sect of the Quakers to be by far the most considerable of any that divide from us, in case the Quakerism that is generally held be the same with that which Mr. Barclay has delivered to the world."

When Voltaire read the "Apology," he gave as his verdict that it was "as good as a book of its kind could possibly be," and written in the best Church Latin with which he was acquainted. Besides Robert Barclay's own English version, it has been translated into Dutch, Danish, German, Spanish and French, and parts of it into Arabic, and has been read by all classes of readers. If Robert Barclay had been nothing more than a scholar and theologian, his work would have only had an academic value. But he himself chose to be known not as a scholar, but as a "Servant of Jesus Christ," and it is for this reason that his work is a living force to-day.

Besides the scanty biography written by his son, there are not many records of his doings. No portrait of him is known to exist, we have no details of his personal appearance, and, with two or three exceptions, no one seems to have recorded his spoken words. But we

know that he was a man with many
friends, and greatly beloved; highly
gifted, with wide sympathies, and great
joy in life.

CHAPTER II.

Early Years.

On the 23rd of December, 1648, Robert Barclay was born at Gordonstown, in the North of Scotland. His father, David Barclay, was famous as a soldier; he had gone abroad early, and had distinguished himself on the Protestant side in the Thirty Years' War. He returned to Scotland at the outbreak of the Civil War, and rose to the rank of colonel in the Covenanting army.

Robert Barclay's mother, Catherine, the daughter of Sir Robert Gordon, was a member of the famous Gordon clan, which was allied by marriage to the ruling House of Stuart, she was third cousin to Charles I.[1] Her ancestors had been among the first Scotch Reformers and prominent theologians of their day.

[1] See p. 119.

David Barclay was married on the
26th of January, 1648, and for some years
his home was at Gordonstown with
his wife's parents, and there Robert
Barclay's childhood was spent. Gordonstown House lies in a sheltered hollow,
six miles north of Elgin, and one mile
from the shore of the Moray Firth. The
wings of the original building still remain. The walls are eight feet thick,
the roof is surmounted by turrets, secret
staircases and passages abound. It is a
gloomy place, but the scenery around is
beautiful. For generations this region
has been celebrated for its rich crops,
and its genial climate. To the south
rises the blue range of the Grampians,
and in sight of these mountains the
greater part of Robert Barclay's life was
spent.

He was the eldest of a family of
five children, three boys and two girls.
His uncle, Sir Ludovic Gordon, with his

wife and eight children also lived at Gordonstown. The eldest son of this family was a few years older than his cousin Robert.

Robert Barclay was a month old when Charles I. was executed at Whitehall, " a treacherous, treasonable, and bloody act," wrote the Chronicler of his mother's family, Gilbert Gordon. A year and a half later, Charles II. landed from Holland at Garmouth, ten miles from Gordonstown. The Gordon clan, with all the Royalists of the north, gathered to do him homage. He hoped, with Scotland's help, to gain his kingdom, and his Calvinist subjects believed that he would establish the supremacy of their religion. But these hopes were doomed to disappointment. He was driven from the country after crushing defeat, and his early schooling in Presbyterianism only served to give him a loathing for the whole system.

Robert Barclay, too, was schooled in the doctrines and practices of the Kirk, and with the same result. Years afterwards he wrote of these early experiences :

"Truth Triumphant," Vol. III., p. 186.

"My first education from my infancy up fell among the strictest sort of Calvinists, those of our country being generally acknowledged to be the severest of that sect, in the heat of zeal surpassing not only Geneva, (from whence they derive their pedigree) but all other the Reformed Churches abroad. . . So that some of the French Protestants being upbraided with the fruits of this zeal, as it appeared in John Knox . . and others, do . . . alledge, the superabundance thereof to proceed . . . from the violent complexion of our countrymen."

His father was not a strong supporter of the Kirk. He was a man of vigorous and independent mind and he was not prepared to accept the ruling of the Presbytery in the detailed affairs of his life.

In 1653 this entry was made in the Synod
Records of Moray:—" David Barclay,
sonne-in-law to Sir Robert Gordon, has
professedlie declined from the doctrine
and discipline of this Kirk, denying it
to be a Kirk. The Synod ordains him
to be processed." In spite of every
attempt of the Kirk to win him back,
David Barclay pursued an independent
path.

Robert, his eldest son, soon showed
signs of unusual ability. He was sent
to the best schools in the neighbourhood
of Gordonstown, but his father decided
that he should have better educational
advantages than these could offer, and
he sent the boy to Paris to be educated
under the charge of his uncle and name-
sake, Robert Barclay, who was Rector
of the Scots' Theological College there.
This institution had been founded in the
Middle Ages by a Bishop of Morayshire,
to enable intelligent lads from remote

country parts to benefit by the advantages of an education in Paris. Robert
Barclay, being a native of Morayshire,
had a natural claim to these privileges.
The usual age at which students were
admitted was fifteen ; however, perhaps
through the influence of his uncle, Robert
was admitted when scarcely more than
a child. People were attracted to Paris
from all parts of Europe by the brilliant
court of Louis XIV., and by the famous
University. The aim of the Scots' Theological College at this time was to prepare
its students for returning as Roman
Catholic Missionaries to their native land.
While in Paris Robert went through the
course of an ordinary liberal education
of his time. He studied classics, rhetoric
and divinity. He was taught fencing
and "other gentlemanly accomplish-
ments." But the atmosphere of the
College was the atmosphere of the Church
of Rome. He wrote of this time :

"Truth
Triumph-
ant."
Vol. III.,
p. 186.
" My tender years, and immature capacity
not being able to withstand and resist the
insinuations, that were used to proselyte me
to that way, I became quickly defiled with
the pollutions thereof ; and continued therein
for a time."

The sights with which he grew familiar
during these years were the grey towers
of the Cathedral of Nôtre Dame, the steep
street leading up from the river bank to
the church of St. Etienne du Mont, one of
the most beautiful in Paris, and close to
which was the narrow Rue des Amandiers,
now Rue de la Place, where the College
stood. This student life in Paris was
much to Robert's taste. He tells us :

"Truth
Triumph-
ant."
Vol. III.,
p. 187.
" From my very childhood I was very
ambitious of knowledge, and by a certain
felicity of understanding (I think I may say
without vanity) successful beyond many of
my equals in age."

He soon became conspicuous among
the   other   students,   and   particularly

distinguished himself in debate. His uncle was very proud of this promising pupil. But Robert's Paris life was suddenly cut short.

His mother fell ill at Gordonstown, and an intense longing for her boy seized her. She had always dreaded the influence of a Roman Catholic atmosphere for him. Now she begged her husband that he might be brought home. This David Barclay promised. His wife died in the spring of 1663, and shortly afterwards he started for Paris. Lady Gordon, Robert's grandmother, waited eagerly for his return. She had been the first to notice great promise in the child. David Barclay's other children were in her charge during his absence. She wrote[1] urging her son-in-law to let no thought of worldly gain prevent him carrying out his intention to bring Robert home again. Bound by his promise,

[1] See p. 121.

David Barclay stood firm against all the arguments of his brother. The Rector said that if the boy remained at the College, he should become his heir, and thus enter into an influential position, while in the meantime his talents would have every opportunity of being fully developed. When Robert himself was appealed to about returning to Scotland with David Barclay, he replied simply, " He is my father and must be obeyed." So father and son set off together on the long journey north. Robert was fifteen years old when he reached his home.

Presbyterians and Roman Catholics had tried to influence and determine his opinions.

" Truth Triumph- ant," Vol. III., p. 187.

" In both these Sects," he tells us, " I had abundant occasion to receive impressions contrary to . . [the] principle of Love."

Of the years which followed, he wrote:

" Truth Triumph- ant," Vol. III., p. 187.

"I kept myself free from joining with any sort of people ; though I took liberty to hear several ; and my converse was most with those, that inveigh much against judging, and such kind of severity. . . . Which latitude may perhaps be esteemed the other extreme opposite to the preciseness of these other sects; whereby I also received an opportunity to know what usually is pretended on that side likewise. . . ."

When Robert was seventeen years old his father was imprisoned in Edinburgh Castle, charged with having held office during the Commonwealth. Charles II. was now established on the throne, and bent on compelling the Scots to accept the ecclesiastical system which was dear to himself because it established his own supremacy, and hateful to them because it cut at the root of the Presbyterian system which many of them valued more than their own lives. The first open rebellion against these

innovations occurred in the year of David
Barclay's arrest. It was true that he
had held important civil posts under the
Commonwealth, but he had broken with
the Covenanting party because their
religious ideas differed from his own.
He had been repelled by the bigotry
within the Kirk, as well as by the bitter
animosity of the sects without it. He
had noticed that each of these laid claim
to be the true Church, and in turn, as
opportunity offered, persecuted the
others for holding that same opinion.
David Barclay was a man of exceptional
force. As a soldier his commanding
stature and prodigious strength of arm,
as well as his military skill, had made
him a marked man. He sat in two of
Cromwell's Parliaments, and in the
administration of local government in his
native county of Kincardine he had
earned great renown. Another and
more compelling power was yet to be

disclosed in him. Hitherto he had not shown himself a strong partisan. Now he had turned back to first principles as a possible way of escape from the wrangling of the sects, and in the person of Christ he had found a leader before whom he was prepared to lay down all. While in London he had often heard of the Quakers, and had been attracted by the principles they taught, as well as by their manner of life. He noticed that they refused to fight even those who might be called their enemies, and that they loved one another. These two facts struck him as very remarkable, and he decided that these must be the true followers of Christ upon earth if there were any such. In this state of mind he found himself thrust into a cell of Edinburgh Castle with one other man for his fellow prisoner. This man was John Swinton,[1] a Quaker. Like the rest of his sect, he had turned

[1] John Swinton was an ancestor of Sir Walter Scott.

his imprisonment into a means of spreading his own belief. It was the contagiousness of Quakerism which made it one of the most difficult problems for the authorities to deal with. The Privy Council had just appointed a special Commission to enquire into the best methods of suppressing this most pernicious sect. Swinton had been ordered solitary confinement, but the prison was overcrowded, so David Barclay shared his cell.

Robert Barclay was in Edinburgh during the early part of his father's imprisonment, and had leave to visit him. But this leave was soon withdrawn, for the Governor of the Castle discovered that the boy was getting infected with the Quaker venom. Thus left to his own devices, and having tasted the spiritual food that Swinton, the Quaker, had given him, and for which he had craved, the boy decided to go to one of the gatherings of these despised people. There were several Quaker meetings in Edinburgh at this time, though the Privy Council had done all in its power to suppress them. Any one who sanctioned such a gathering on his premises was liable to punishment. All repressive measures were tried upon the Quakers themselves ; but fines, imprisonment, confiscation of goods, ostracism, and ridicule failed to deter the valiant among them. As a rule the weak in faith and courage grew stronger under this treatment. If their Meeting House was closed to them, the Quakers gathered for worship in the open street. There they succeeded in preserving their aloofness from all disturbing elements, and people were forced to own that they were upheld by some power that could not be reached by human interference. Robert Barclay has left us a description of the impression made upon him by the first

Quaker meetings which he attended. He wrote :

" Apology," XI., §7.

" When I came into the silent assemblies of God's people, I felt a secret power among them, which touched my heart, and as I gave way unto it, I found the evil weakening in me, and the good raised up, and so I became thus knit and united into them, hungering more and more after the increase of this power and life, whereby I might feel myself perfectly redeemed."

He was eighteen years old when he joined the Society of Friends.

CHAPTER III

URY

IT was no easy matter to join the Society of Friends at that time. David Barclay, who had also declared himself a Quaker, did not regain his liberty for four years. He petitioned for his release, and his petition was forwarded to the King. The reply sent down to the Privy Council was as follows :—

Register of the Privy Council of Scotland. Third Series, Vol. III., p. 615.

" We did see the petition of David Barclay, which though it be of ane unusual straine, yet, if he will signe such a bond and security, as the uther persons did who were committed with him, wee doe allow you to grant him his liberty, bot if he refuse, then you shall remove him to some other prison, for we will not have our Castle of Edinborough made a prison."

" . . . Subscribitur by His Majesty's command, "Lauderdale."

But David Barclay refused to sign the bond, and accordingly, after nearly three years' imprisonment in Edinburgh, he was ordered to transport himself to Montrose. In the meantime he had sent Robert to live at Ury, near the fishing village of Stonehaven. This was a large estate, which had recently come into his possession. It consisted of forest-land, gorse-covered up-land, and pasturage. Again Robert's home lay near the foothills of the Grampians, and within easy reach of the sea. His companion there was David Falconer, a young Quaker, whom David Barclay had chosen to be his factor.

Affairs at Ury were in great disorder, and a further petition on David Barclay's behalf states that unless he were allowed "to make some shift for his own and his children's maintenance, he or they shall starve," so David Barclay was allowed to go where he liked in Montrose,

Register of the Privy Council of Scotland. Third Series, Vol. II., p. 457.

but forbidden to leave the town. The magistrates were advised to " be carefull no quaikers frequent his own company, except his own sone."

Robert Barclay continued his studies during these years. He wanted to prepare himself to answer some of the attacks made on the Quakers. He wrote :

" Truth Triumphant," Vol. I., p. 324.

" Some will have us to be Foolish, Mad Creatures ; others to be deep, subtle Politicians ; some to be illiterate, ignorant Fellows ; others to be Learned, Cunning Jesuits under a mere Vizard. . . Sometimes we are a Disorderly Confused Rabble, leaving everyone to do as they list, against all good Order and Government ; at other Times we are so much for Order, as we admit not Men to exercise the Liberty of their own Judgments. Thus are our Reputations tossed by the Envy of our Adversaries. . . [who] save us the Pains while they Refute one another."

His first attempt at controversial

URY.

writing was in correspondence with his uncle, George Gordon, a Calvinist.

Robert Barclay was often in Aberdeen. He was much attracted by a young Quakeress, Christian Molleson by name. Her father was a baillie of that town. When he was twenty-one, Robert wrote her the following letter :—

" 28th of $\frac{1}{mo}$ 1669

" Dear Friend,

" Having for some time past had it several times upon my mind to have saluted thee in this manner of writing, and to enter into a literal correspondence with thee, so far as thy freedom could allow, I am glad that this small occasion hath made way for the beginning of it. The love of thy converse, the desire of thy friendship, the sympathy of thy way, and the meekness of thy spirit, have often, as thou mayest have observed, occasioned me to take frequent opportunity to have the benefit of thy company . . . but beyond and before all I can say, in the fear of the Lord, that I have received a charge from Him to love thee. . . I am sure it will be our great gain so to be kept, that all of us may abide in the pure love of God; in the sense of drawings whereof we can only discern and know how to love one another. In the present flowings thereof I have truly solicited thee, desiring and expecting that in the same thou mayst feel and judge.

"ROBERT BARCLAY."

A year later Robert Barclay and Christian Molleson were married at a Quaker Meeting held in her father's house. No priest officiated. The two became man and wife simply by declaring their love to each other and their dependence on God. But when it was known in the town what had taken place, all Aberdeen was in an uproar. Nothing of the kind had ever happened before. The clergy declared that their authority was slighted, and that Robert must be summoned before the Privy Council; the laity were horrified at the brazen

effrontery of the Quakers, and the mob,
ever ready on the smallest pretext for
excitement, set upon the Friends, who
were peaceably assembling for their
Monthly Meeting. But the tumult sub-
sided as suddenly as it arose. No
proceedings were taken. The Friends'
record of the time states simply "that
the matter was so over-ruled of the Lord,
that they had never power to put their
summons in executione." Shortly after
the wedding, David Barclay, who for
sometime had been a prisoner upon his
own estate at Ury, obtained his full
liberty. He built Ury House, which for
200 years was the home of his descen-
dants. It was a grim, formidable
building, with massive walls, and vaulted
floors. It stood near the stream which
traverses the estate. He also built a
Meeting House, in spite of having been
expressly forbidden by the Privy Council
"to keep Quaker Meetings." But he

preferred to obey his own conscience, and take the consequences. An increasing number of his tenants and neighbours met there week by week.

Robert was twenty-two when he published his first tract in defence of Quakerism. He called it "Truth Cleared of Calumnies." In it he states the aim which he set before himself throughout life: "To answer to the good that is in all, and to starve and not to feed the evil in any." The following year he published two more pamphlets.

Shortly after this, Robert Barclay, impelled by some inward voice, made a public testimony in the streets of Aberdeen, where he appeared clad in sackcloth with ashes upon his head,[1] crying to the people to repent. Though many of the early Friends felt called to express their message in symbolic form, Robert

[1] As a child he had often seen penitents in this guise at the Kirk door.

Barclay's instance is a peculiar one. There was nothing of the fanatic in his nature. But one morning the strange call came to him, and the record of what followed can only be told in his own words :

"Truth Triumph-ant." Vol. 1, p. 195.

". . . The Command of the Lord concerning this thing came unto me that very Morning, as I awakened, and the Burthen thereof was very great ; yea, seemed almost insupportable unto me, (for such a thing, until that very Moment, had never entered me before, not in the most remote Consideration.) And some, whom I called to declare to them this thing, can bear Witness, how great was the Agony of my Spirit, how I besought the Lord with Tears, that this Cup might pass away from me ! Yea, how the Pillars of my Tabernacle were shaken, and how exceedingly my Bones trembled, until I freely gave up unto the Lord's Will."

This is the only occasion when he

adopted the symbolic form for his message. As time went on he spoke less of the doctrine of repentance, and more of " Gift of the Father's Love."

" Truth
Triumph-
ant,"
Vol. III.
p. 247.

His eldest son, who was called Robert, was born at Ury in April, 1672. At the close of the same year, Robert Barclay left home in the dead of winter with his father's friend, John Swinton, and rode over to Montrose. " A pretty town, with a safe harbour," as a contemporary described it. There was a Friends' Meeting in Montrose, but almost all its members had just suffered imprisonment. They were now released, and met together on this December Sunday to give thanks for their deliverance. Robert Barclay and Swinton joined them. Hardly had the meeting begun when the officers appeared at the door and fresh arrests were made. Robert Barclay and Swinton went before the magistrates to plead for their friends, but were them-

Thomas
Tucker,
1655.

selves convicted and imprisoned in the
Tolbooth of Montrose. While in prison,
Robert Barclay wrote a letter to the
magistrates of the town setting forth
the wrong he and his fellow prisoners
were undergoing. He stated that the
law by which they had been committed
was really directed against those who
endangered the peace of the realm. He
urged that the Quakers were loyal subjects, who asked nothing but leave to
meet together and worship God in their
own way.

" As for us," he concluded, " we are not
afraid of you, nor ashamed of our testimony,
and you cannot vanquish us. . . We are,
as regards our testimony and for its sake,
well contented, well pleased, well satisfied,
to be here ; our bonds are not grievous to
us."

His letter appears to have had weight,
and early the following year all the
prisoners were released. Robert Barclay

returned to his work with redoubled zeal. He was twenty-eight years old when the "Apology" was written.

While he was busy in his study, his father, David Barclay, was closely occupied with the business of his estate. As laird, he exercised judicial power over his tenants and was much respected and loved, but as a Quaker he was exposed to constant insult and abuse.[1] Yet " it was remarked that none suffered those indignities with greater calmness."

Christian and Robert Barclay had seven children.

Alexander Jaffray, one of the Aberdeen Friends who was a frequent visitor at Ury, and a close friend of the family, writes of " the beauty, good order, [and] holiness that shined therein, I can say to my refreshment and many others, as in a quiet habitation."

Genealogical Account of the Barclays of Ury, p. 42.

[1] See Whittier's " Barclay of Ury."

CHAPTER IV

LETTERS

In 1676 Robert Barclay went to Holland, taking the manuscript of the " Apology " with him. This work was first published in Amsterdam. He then continued his journey to Herford in Westphalia, where he visited a distant relation, Elizabeth, Princess Palatine of the Rhine. She was the daughter of Frederick, Elector Palatine, who was son-in-law to James I. of England. She was a Protestant, an earnest student, and a woman of wide sympathies. A close friendship sprang up between them. Robert Barclay left her a copy of the " Apology," and she made him the bearer of a letter to her brother, Prince Rupert, whom she urged to use all his influence in England, to procure the release of Friends then in prison. When Robert reached London he heard that his father had been arrested, and was then confined in the Tolbooth in Aberdeen. He obtained an audience with the King, and presented to him a petition on behalf of the prisoners, asking for "some present relief to those harmless sufferers, to prevent that utter ruin, which, in all probability will attend so many of them that live by their labour and trade." He also presented the King with a copy of the "Apology." This work is prefaced by a letter addressed to Charles II.

"It is far from me," wrote Robert Barclay, "to use this epistle as an engine to flatter thee, the usual design of such works; and therefore I can neither dedicate it to thee, nor crave thy patronage, as if thereby I might have more confidence to present it to the world, or be more hopeful of its success . . . But I found it upon my spirit to take occasion

to present this book unto thee ; that as thou
hast been often warned by several . . .
who are inhabitants of England ; so thou
mayest not want a seasonable advertisement from a member of thy ancient kingdom
of Scotland."

He reminded the King of the
peaceableness and loyalty of his Quaker
subjects, their courage under persecution, and the faithfulness with which
they had " discharged their consciences,"
for "they have not spared to admonish,
exhort, and reprove thee," and continued :

" If thou wilt allow thyself so much time
as to read this, [the " Apology "] thou
mayest find how consonant their principles
are both to scripture, truth, and right
reason."

He concluded by warning Charles
against "the flattering of court parasites"
and urging him to apply himself " to
that Light of Christ, which shineth in
thy conscience."   Charles does not seem

to have resented this plainness of
speech, and Robert Barclay continued
to be received at Court. He wrote in
August to one of his friends :[1]

"I have at last, after long and tedious
attendance, near finished my business ; for
the Duke of Lauderdale tells me yesterday,
he has received order to give me a letter to
the Council in Scotland in order to grant
Friends their liberty, which he has promised
to give me to-morrow, so that I propose
in two or three days to be going homewards."

He also wrote to the Princess Elizabeth
during these negotiations.

"London, 24th of $\frac{4}{mo}$ 1676.
"Dear Friend,
"The sense and constant remembrance
which I entertain in my Spirit of that good
opportunity which it pleased the Lord to
minister unto us when together, would long
e'er now have engaged me to write unto thee,
but that I was not willing to do any thing

[1] Stephen Crisp.

in the forwardness of my own Spirit. . .
The Lord seems to have laid a particular
care and concern upon me which I am very
willing to answer, for He hath kindled that
love in my heart for thee which I shall not
adventure to express lest I might seem to
exceed. . . I shall be glad to hear from
thee as thou finds true freeness to let me know
how things are with thee, let these transmit
the remembrance of my true and unfeigned
love to the Countess of Hornes,[1] I hope she
hath held her resolutions of learning to read
and understand English, which it may please
the Lord to bless unto her. I delivered thy
letter to thy Brother, who was civill to me,
I also took occasion from thence to employ
him to be assisting to me in ane address I
Intend to make to the King in behalf of my
Father, and about forty more of our Friends
that are about some months ago Imprisoned
in Scotland for Conscience sake, in which he
promised his Concurrence; if it prove success-
full it is well, if not, it is well also we must

---

[1] One of the ladies in attendance upon the Princess.

be contented to suffer, and I shall go home
cheerfully, willing to partake with them
of their bonds, I intend to send thee some
books which I hope may be usefull unto thee,
but above all I recommend thee to that
inward word of Grace in which thou can
read thyself and learn to know the Lord,
in which pure and fruitfull knowledge that
thou may more and more advance is the
earnest desire of

" Thy Assured Friend in the love of Jesus,
" R. BARCLAY."

Princess Elizabeth wrote the following
reply :

" July $\frac{21}{31}$ 1676.
" My dear Friend in our Saviour Jesus Christ.
" I have received your Letter dated the
24th of June this day. . . Your memory is
dear unto me, so are your lines and your
exhortations very necessary, I confess myself still spiritually very poor and naked and
all my happiness is that I doe know that I
am so, and that whatsoever I have studied
and learned heretofore is but dirt in com-

parison to the true knowledge of Christ. I confess also my infidelity to this light heretofore by suffering myself to be conducted by false politick lights now that I have sometimes a small glimpse of the true light I do not attend it as I should being drawn away by the works of my calling which must be done, and (as your swift English hounds) I often overrun my sent being called back when it is too late. Let not this make you less earnest in prayers for me, you see I need them, your Letters will be always welcom to me, so will your Friends if any please to visit me. I should admire God's providence if my Brother could be a means of releasing your Father and forty more in Scotland having promised to do his best I know he will perform it he has ever been true to his word and you shall find me with the grace of our Lord a true friend,

" ELIZABETH."

" P.S.—The Countess of Hornes sends you her most hearty commendations, she has not had time to learn English having imployed it in more necessary works since God hath

visited this Family with many sick of smallpox
and contagious Feavers of which she has had
a care not considering the Infection, amongst
the rest there was a Servant of hers very
desperately sick of whom she had ane especiall
care deeming her to be also a Sister in Christ
who did draw great comfort out of the books
you left here."

Knowing of her interest in the prisoners,
Robert Barclay kept Princess Elizabeth
in touch with the progress of the negotiations for their release. From Edinburgh
he wrote to her as follows :

                              " 6th of September, 1676.
" Dear Friend,
    " Last night thy acceptable letter came to
my hands, in which my Spirit was refreshed,
in a sence that the Lord continueth his love
to thee. . .   I doubt not but thy Brother
would have kept his word in speaking to the
King in my behalf, but it so happened that
at that time he had a sore legg (of which he is
since recovered) so that I could not make
use of him, with no small difficulty I obtained

a kind of recommendation from the King to the council of state, but such is the opposition and enmity of the world's spirit against us, and the Influence of the chief Bishops who sit in Council, that no release for the Prisoners could be obtained, so that they must patiently suffer till the Lord in his own time work their deliverance, who will suffer them to continue no longer there than is good for their souls and his own glory and indeed they have great reason to be contented, for the glory and heavenly majesty of the Lord doth singularly every day appear among them, and the virtuous Life of Jesus doth often flow among them as a mighty stream . . . Thus are shut up together forty-two men in one great room who not of self will nor their own choice but by the providence of God are placed for a time together in a heavenly community. . . . I this day take my Journey towards them, not doubting but I shall be taken and shut up with them and with all cheerfulness of spirit am prepared to partake wt them of their bonds, not doubting but I shall also

share of their Joys . . . It will be a
very refreshful and comfortable to me in
my Prison to hear of thee, for thy Prosperity
and Increase in the truth is desired by me
as that of my own Soul . . .

        " Thy faithful friend,

                " R. BARCLAY."

A few months after his return home,
Robert Barclay was arrested. He was
confined in the Tolbooth[1] at Aberdeen.
The cell was dark and crowded. Its
windows were boarded up, to prevent the
Quaker prisoners addressing the crowds
who gathered in the market-place below.
But the preachers were undaunted, and
their voices still reached the ears of the
people, although they themselves could
not be seen. Robert Barclay was busy
writing, and was very happy. One of his

---

[1] The old Tolbooth Tower, and some of the original
cells still remain, and form a part of the Court House
Building. The Curfew bell in the Tower was rung daily
at 5 a.m. and 8 p.m. This custom was discontinued in
1902, but it is still possible to hear the note with which
the prisoners were familiar.

fellow prisoners remarked that he was
"a man . . . among many for even-
ness of spirit." It was during this time
of imprisonment that he wrote his treatise
on "Universal Love." He also wrote
many letters.

Hearing of his imprisonment, Princess
Elizabeth wrote to him, "I am sure
that the Captivers are more Captive
than you." She wrote as follows to
her brother on his behalf:—

"Herford,
"Dec. 19th, 1676.

"Dear Brother,

"I have written to you some months ago,
by Robert Barclay, who passed this way,
and hearing I was your sister, desired to
speak with me. I knew him to be a Quaker
by his hat, and took occasion to inform myself
of all their opinions: and finding they were
to submit to Magistrates in real things,
omitting the ceremonial, I wished in my heart
the King might have many such subjects:

and since I have heard that notwithstanding
his Majesty's most gracious letters in his
behalf to the Council of Scotland, he has been
clapt up in prison with the rest of his
friends, and they threaten to hang them, at
least those they call preachers among them,
unless they subscribe their own banishment;
and this upon a law made against other
sects, that appeared armed for the maintenance of their heresy, which goes directly
against the principles of those which are
ready to suffer all that can be inflicted, and
still love and pray for their enemies. Therefore, dear Brother, if you can do anything
to prevent their destruction, I doubt not but
you will do an action, acceptable to God
Almighty, and conducive to the service of
your Royal Master : for the Presbyterians
are their main enemies, to whom they are
an eyesore, as being witnesses against all their
violent ways. I care not though his Majesty
see my letter : it is written out of no less
an humble affection for him, than most
sensible compassion of the innocent sufferers. You will act according to your

own discretion, and I beseech you still consider me as,

" Yours,

" Elizabeth."

" A Monr. le Prince
　　Rupert à Londres."

The coming of letters must have been a welcome interlude to the long dark days in prison. The following is Robert Barclay's reply to one from Princess Elizabeth :

" Abdⁿ Prison,

" 24th Xber, 1676.

" Dear Friend,

" Thy letter in Answer to mine of the 6th of September came yesternight to my hand and was very acceptable unto me in my present bonds, my fervent desires always remain for thee to hear that thou continueth under a sence of thy present condition, and seeth the need thou has to partake of the Spirituall riches of Christs Kingdom which are more desirable than all the world, this

is good in its place but thou must not satisfie
thyself to abide here, but must apply thyself
to that divine grace and light that hath shewn
thee thy poverty in which there is power to
make thee rich, if thou can receive and
suffer it to dwell richly in thee, I confess
that so needful inward Silence is hard to
the naturall mind especially to those who
have enriched their Spirits with great variety
of notions and have laboured to deck themselves with the wisdom and knowledge of
this world, thy eminency wherein though it
commended thee to the world renders now
that which is most needfull so difficult for
thee and makes that thy Friend[1] because of
her greater simplicity and less attainments
in these things has a readier access to possess
and enjoy the naked truth which for this
cause of old was more readily received by
poor fishermen and simple women than by
the great Rabbies and wise Greeks, yet thy
difficulties are not so great, nor thy encum-
brances so Invincible but that the grace of
God which has appeared unto thee and has

[1] The Countess of Hornes.

really touched thee with a sence of thy
condition is sufficient for thee, therefore
beware that the Enemy do not betray thee
(after the Lord hath thus awakened thee)
as if sufficient grace were not given thee
to deliver thee from all thy temptations for
God as he is powerfull so he is willing thou
should overcome and his Grace will not be
to thee in vain unless thou make it so by
unfaithfulness, in that seed and light that
has appeared to thee, there is strength to
deliver thee from all though the appearance
of it be small yet there is might in it as it is
received therefore it is compared to a grain
of mustard seed. Remember that parable.
I know no calling (however it were lawful
otherways) that ought to divert thee from
this so necessary a business, the Kingdom
of God ought to be sought after in the first
part, though it were with the neglect of other
matters which will be abundantly made up
otherways and caring for the better part,
it matters not though other matters be
disregarded for a season. For this man
was commended of the Lord Jesus, and

indeed when the Lord touches the heart of
any to draw them out of the Spirit of this
world there is great retirement and ab-
straction both of mind and body necessary
for a season, because of the soul's weakness
at such a time and its capacity to be
entangled with any diversion, therefore let
me not only seriously advise thee. . . to
draw near to the Lord in the small appearance of his seed in thy heart and for that end
abstract thyself from the multiplicity of
thy outward affairs though thou should
leave undone not only all things that are
superfluous, but even some things that may
appear to thee at present to be needfull in
that respect, and afterwards when through
such retirement to be more acquainted
and so more distinctly to perceive and discern
the witness of God in thy soul . . . thou
will be more capable clearly to distinguish
betwixt the pretious and the vile and more
enabled to forsake the one and follow the
other. If upon a pressing outward bussiness
or to visit a relation or friend after the flesh
thou can retire thyself for a season from these

outward diversions far more ought thou to
disentangle thyself when the Lord calls for
it by the awakening of his seed in thy heart
for the redemption of thy soul, two things
are therefore absolutely needful . . . to
wit, faith and obedience, faith in the measure
and manifestation of the light and grace that
hath appeared so as not to be befooled by the
Enemy and kept under his bonds through
a faithless persuasion that the temptations
and difficulties are too great or too strong,
for any grace already obtained, and obedience
in the things already clearly discovered
especially in acts of forbearance in whatever
is seen not so profitable or acceptable, and
not a deferring to obey in things already
seen through a hope and foolish desire to
see and understand more, this is to resemble
the unprofitable servant that hid his talent,
and judged God a hard master, it is needful
then to believe in the power and virtue of
God's grace received, not doubting but as
more is needed it will be added, and to obey
in all things already manifested, not medling
in things as yet not seen. . . I hope thou

will take in good part my fredom herein
which proceedeth from pure love and ane
earnest desire I have that thou may go on
so as not to loose the glorious prize that is
set before thee, which is better than ane
earthly crown.   My soul breaths to the Lord
for thee that this may be thy portion, for the
obtaining whereof I with my Brethren do at
present contentedly suffer these bonds
though we see no way of outward deliverance, not doubting but the Lord will bring
it about in his own time.   In the belief
whereof is at present patiently satisfied thy
assured friend,   "BARCLAY."

It was a relief to Robert Barclay to
find that his friend did not resent these
exhortations.   His next letter begins as
follows :—

                "Aberdeen Prison,
           "5th of the month March, 1677.
"Dear and well beloved Elizabeth,
    "By thine of the 19th of the last month
I receive with gladness the renewed testi-
mony of thy love and friendship. . . It is

far from me to require of any, far less of thee,
to do anything meerly upon my persuasion.
My dear friend the Lord give thee a
clear understanding of these things who
knows I use this freedom with thee not to
overdrive thee but of pure love."

The Princess succeeded in persuading
her brother, Prince Rupert, to petition for
Robert Barclay's release. He regained
his freedom after four months in prison
through the intervention of the Duke of
York. Princess Elizabeth wrote, "I do
love the Duke of York for it."

Soon after, Robert Barclay joined a
little party of Friends who had planned a
missionary journey to Holland and
Germany. The party included George
Fox, the veteran leader of the Society,
and William Penn ; this is the only time
when we hear of the three Quaker leaders
being together. The Friends all attended
meeting in Harwich before starting.
The packet boat sailed at one in the

morning for Briel. In spite of "fair brisk wind" and the "fresh gale" which they encountered on the North Sea, two meetings were held on board during the day with the Dutch and French passengers. By evening the boat lay becalmed three miles from the Dutch Coast. Knowing that one of the Dutch Friends had arranged to meet them that night in Briel, William Penn and Robert Barclay hired two sailors to row them ashore in a small boat. But the gates of the town were shut before they reached it, and they were obliged to spend the night in the boat. Next morning the travellers reached Rotterdam. After spending a few days in Holland, where many Meetings were held, Robert Barclay with Penn, and two other Friends, turned south towards Herford. This journey, partly by boat, partly by the common post wagon, lasted four days. At this time France with English support

was waging offensive war in the Nether-
lands, and the country was over-run with
troops.[1] But the travellers spent a peace-
ful week-end at Herford, in mid June
of the year 1677. The little town, with
its seven Church spires, lies in rich
meadow country at the foot of the Teuto-
burger Hills. They lodged at an inn
in the town, and spent a great part of the
day at the Castle, with the Princess,
who welcomed them warmly. Her sympathy with Friends had grown since
Robert Barclay's first visit. She was
now abbess of one of the ancient religious
foundations of the town, which, at the
time of the Reformation, had been
allowed to continue as a Protestant
institution. Meetings were held at the
Castle, with the household of the Princess.
The four Friends spent Sunday morning
quietly at the inn. In the afternoon,
all the townspeople of Herford were

[1] See p. 107.

invited to the Castle for a final Meeting,
before the travellers went on their way.

Robert Barclay returned direct to
England, while the other Friends continued their journey through Germany.
Speaking of his travels with Robert,
Penn said "the apprehension. . . I
had of him was this, he loved the truth
and way of God . . . and was not
ashamed of it before men ; but bold and
able in maintaining it ; sound in judgment, sound in argument, cheerful in
travails and sufferings."

His first effort on reaching England
was to try and obtain the release of his
friends then in prison. On his way north
from London, Robert Barclay wrote the
following letter to Princess Elizabeth :

Testimony
to the
memory
of Robert
Barclay.

" Theobalds, near London,

" 12th of $\frac{7}{mo}$ 1677.

" Dear Friend,

" By thy letter of the last of the month
past, I understand of the friends being with

thee ; and was refreshed by the account
they gave me of thy kind and Christian
entertainment of them (they having overtaken
me in Holland). God will not be wanting
to reward thy love, as well as to encrease the
same. Finding no ready passage streight for
Scotland, I came over here ; and albeit
I had no great expectation of success, I
resolved once more to try thy Cusen the
Duke of York. So I told him, that I understand from Scotland, that notwithstanding
Lauderdale was there and had promised,
ere he went, to doe something, yet our
Friends bonds was rather Increased ; and
that now there was only one thing to be done,
which I desired of him, and that was, to write
effectually to the Duke of Lauderdale, in
that stile wherein Lauderdale might understand that he was serious in the bussiness,
and did really intend the thing he write
concerning should take effect ; which I knew
he might do, and I supposed the other would
answer, which, if he would do, I must acknow-
ledge as a great kindness ; but if he did
write, and not in that manner, so that the

other might not suppose him to be serious,
I would rather he should excuse himself the
trouble ; desiring withall to excuse my plain
manner of dealing, as being different from
the Court way of soliciting : all which he
seemed to take in good part, and said he
would so write, as I desired, for my Father
and me, but not for the generall, so he hath
given me a letter : whether it may prove
effectual or not, I cannot determine, but
of this thou may hear of hereafter. I am
now entered into my Journey, and intend to
pass by the way of Ragly. . .

"Thy Real and unfeigned friend,

"R. BARCLAY."

Princess Elizabeth remonstrated with
Robert Barclay for what she felt uncalled
for rashness in risking imprisonment. She
wrote :

"It is a cross to me that you will not
make use of the liberty that God miracu-
lously gave you, but will return into Scotland
to be clapt up again into prison, for which
there is neither precept nor example."

Undeterred by this prospect, Robert Barclay pursued his way home. Some time elapsed before he was again " clapped up into prison," and then his confinement was of short duration. His last letter to Princess Elizabeth was written from Rotterdam, a short time before her death.[1]

" 6th of the $\frac{5}{mo.}$ 1679.
" Dear Friend,

" Thou may think strange that after so long a silence, I should now apply myself to answer thy last (which came to my hands at a time when I was under great bodily weakness) for which I will not trouble thee with any further Apology than to assure thee that no want of respect or regard to thee but ane unwillingness to work in mine own will, and a fear in so doing rather to hurt than help thee hath hindered me until now, had I given way to my own Inclinations and to the course of that love which without flattery I can say I have for thee so as to

[1] She died in 1680.

have exprest but the hundred part of that concern which frequently possessed me upon thy account. I have over-charged thee with my letters, but knowing it is not the will of man that bringeth about the work of God, I choosed rather to be silent than forward, but being through a singular occasion come to this country and not having access to make thee a visit I found a true liberty from the Lord in my spirit thus to salute thee, for herein I have peace before God, that I never sought to gather thee nor others to myself but to the Lord, I pretend to be no sect master and disgust all such, my labour is only as ane Ambassadour to Instruct all to be reconciled to God, and I desire no more than to be manifest in the Consciences of those to whom I come that I am such, by the answer of that of God there. . .

" Thy sincere and truly affectionat Friend,
" R. BARCLAY."

CHAPTER V

LAST YEARS

IN 1679 the Ury estate was erected into
a Barony by Royal Charter, and civil
and criminal jurisdiction granted to its
owner, on account of "the many faithful
"services done by Colonel David Barclay
"and his son, the said Robert Barclay,
"to the King and his most Royal
"progenitors in times past." At the close
of the same year James, Duke of York,
became a member of the Scotch Privy
Council. The fiercest time of persecution now began for the Covenanters,
but the Quakers enjoyed comparative
peace. Robert Barclay was a friend of
the Duke's, and was constantly at Holy-
rood in conference with him there.
Robert was not a man to conceal his own

opinions ; Roman Catholicism was hateful to him, and he judged persecution
and cruelty "the worst part of Popery,"
as being most contrary to the teaching of
Christ.   Yet some of his closest friends
"Vindica- were Catholics.   "It hath never agreed,"
tion."
he wrote, "with the notions I have of
"Christian religion to hate these persons."
His work as a controversialist was now
over.   The cause of Quakerism called for a
different kind of service.   These early
Friends are standing proofs of the fact
that the true mystic is essentially practical.   It was not enough for them to
preach the possibility that peace can be
obtained on earth, they must at all costs
labour to establish it.

A body of Friends had purchased the
tract of land in America known as East
Jersey, and were engaged in drawing up
their scheme of government.   In 1682
they invited Robert Barclay to accept
the post of Governor.   This he accepted,

with the condition that he was not bound
to go out to America himself, and might appoint a deputy to represent him there. The
man he chose for this office was Gawen
Lawrie, a Quaker, from London. The
document confirming Robert Barclay's
appointment as Governor states that
" such is his known fidelity and
" capacity, that he has the government
" during life, but that no other Governor,
" after him, shall have it longer than for
" three years." Robert Barclay was much
engrossed with the administration of this
new territory, particularly with the
shipment of suitable men to work the
land and establish the Colony, for Gawen
Lawrie wrote urgently that this was the
greatest need. Robert Barclay saw here
a chance to relieve some of the suffering
in his own land. With the accession of
James II. in 1685 began what was known
as " the Black Year, the Killing time."
Two hundred Covenanters, both men and

women, were confined in the vault of
Dunnottar Castle, which, though outside
the limits of David Barclay's jurisdiction,
was technically included in the Ury Estate.
The Castle stands on a precipitous rock,
almost surrounded by the ocean. It had
been purchased from its owner, the Earl
Marischal, for use as a state prison. The
prisoners were confined under conditions
which were particularly barbarous, even
when judged by the standard of that
time. The tales of horror spread through
the neighbourhood. Some of the prisoners escaped from the vaults where
they were confined; some lost their
lives in the attempt; some were caught
and brought back to endure added
suffering.[1]

Robert Barclay set himself to secure
the release of the survivors, and to help
them in escaping to East Jersey which

[1] The names of those who perished are inscribed on a
stone in Dunottar Churchyard, where Sir Walter Scott
first met " Old Mortality."

was a free land. A letter to his Cousin,
John Gordon, who, being a merchant,
had placed his ships at the disposal of
the would-be emigrants, deals with this
subject.

" To Sir John Gordon,
    " Advocat in Edinburgh,
      " Ury, the 4th of the 1st month, 1684.
" Dear Cousine,
  " I suppose thou has wrott ere now, to
London, to thy brother George, and proposed to him to bring down his veshell here to
cary passengers to East Jersey. I doubt
not but he may make as good a venter that
way as any he can propose, and knows how
to project a retourn for himself. There
will not want passengers, besides those that
fills another ship to be hired, and one that
is goeing from Glasgow with Maryward, which
will be the best way. And besids those
George may carry upon thy brother's accompt
and thines, iff he want, it is but getting men
from Strathnaver, to cary over at a venter,
which is as profitable a commodity as he

can trade in ; the sooner something be done in this the better. I expect also from thee a speedy answere as to that part now in thy optione, that thou will determine it one way or orther, that I may regulate myself accordlie. If George com with his ship so as to be ready to goe about Whitsunday, he will be sure to be full, for the other is to com afterwards. Desir him to call at London to William Bockura, at Little St. Helen's, over against Leathersellar's Hall in Bishopgait Street ; who will give him fuil informatione in what may be needfull for him. So, expecting thy care in this, and that thou will lett no time be lost, which is the chief point in such caises, I rest thy affectionat cousine,

" B."[1]

Robert Barclay was constantly travelling to and from Edinburgh and London, and paid long visits in both places.

George Keith, an old friend of Robert Barclay's, and his colleague in many early

[1] From "Social Life in Former Days." By E. Dunbar Dunbar.

controversies, had established a Friends'
school[1] at Theobalds, fifteen miles north
of London. In that rich wooded district
near Waltham Abbey two old houses are
still standing, built early in the seventeenth century. It was probably in one
of these that George Keith established
his school, and it was this school which
Robert Barclay chose for his eldest son.
The boy, aged eleven, set off with his
parents from Ury in the spring of 1683.
After seeing him settled at Theobalds,
his parents spent the summer in London.
This is the only time we hear of Christian
Barclay being with her husband on one
of his long absences from home. On the
return journey they were attacked by
highway-men, and Robert, the younger,
tells the story in the biography of his
father. Christian Barclay noticed early

[1] George Fox, though himself a man of no education,
had a great belief in the importance of education for
other people. He advocated the founding of schools in
which "everything civil and useful in creation" might
be taught.

"Genealo-
gical
Account
of the
Barclays
of Ury"
p. 78.

that morning that her husband was
" more pensive than usual ; he told her
"that it was his opinion that some un-
"usual trial, or exercise, was to befall
"them that day, but when the affair hap-
"pened he enjoyed a remarkable serenity."
Two other Friends who travelled with
them were robbed, and one was fatally in-
jured, but Robert Barclay was unhurt.
When one of the highway-men attacked
him he took the man by the arm, "very
"calmly asking him how he came to be
"so rude, for he knew his business ; the
"fellow trembling dropped the pistol in
"great surprise, and did not so much as
"search or demand anything from him."
Robert and Christian Barclay waited
to attend the funeral of the murdered
man, and then made their way home.

Early in 1685 Robert Barclay went to
Edinburgh to attend his sister's wedding.
She married Sir Ewen Cameron of
Locheil.   Shortly afterwards her hus-

band was accused of treason, and the
Duke of Gordon seized this chance to
assert a fictitious claim to his lands.   In
this dilemma, Locheil applied to his
brother-in-law, Robert Barclay, who
approached various influential people
on his behalf.   They all said they were
sorry for Locheil's difficulty, but declined to mix themselves up in the
quarrel.   Robert, who was convinced of
the rights of his claim, took up the matter
himself, and urged Locheil to apply
direct to the King.   The negotiations
dragged on for some years involving
Robert Barclay in much correspondence
and considerable difficulty.   In Locheil
himself, he had to combat a shrinking and
retiring temperament, while the case
could only be carried through by courage
and out-spokenness.   Finally his efforts
were successful, his brother-in-law's name
was completely cleared and his lands were
restored to him.

Robert Barclay was often called in to negotiate difficult matters. One of his friends wrote: "He was all along a man "for peace, and an enemy to strife and "dissention. . . A man of deep reach "in his judgment and understanding of "Heavenly things, and also of the things "that concerned him to know of this life "amongst men."

Patrick Living-stone.

It was not only by his pen and his intercession for the prisoners that Barclay was the comforter as well as the councillor of the new Society. His purse was always open to the temporal necessities of those whom fines and imprisonments kept in a state of poverty. His son writes :

"Genea-logical Account of the Barclays of Ury" p. 71.

" He employed himself much in assisting his poor friends, for whom he contributed liberally, as he had done for purchasing a Meeting House, at Aberdeen, about the year 1672, it being mostly bought by his money, and some by his means obtained from Lady Connaway, one of the same persuasion in

England, as the Meeting Records testify,
as doth his own diary,[1] or pocket book, all
wrote with his own hand and preserved in
the family ; wherein he gives a very exact
and particular account of many transactions
of his life until some weeks of his death,
which hath been much assistance to me in
writing this account."

George Fox, who was a close friend
of Robert Barclay's, wrote early in 1686
urging him to come to London to plead
for Friends there, who still suffered dis-
abilities owing to their refusal to take
oaths. But during this year Robert
was closely tied at home ; his youngest
child was born in the spring, and he
passed through a time of anxiety about
his wife's health. In the autumn his
father fell ill. " There be hardly to be
" found one of a thousand like to him, for
" natural vigour of his age," wrote Robert,
but after a fortnight's illness, the old

[1] This record is unfortunately lost.

soldier of Christ " fell asleep like a lamb,
" in remarkable quietness and calmness."
He was buried in the vault of the small
burying ground which he had purchased
for Friends, and which was part of the
Ury Estate. It is called the Houff,
and stands on the top of a low conical
hill overlooking Ury glen, and many miles
of surrounding country. The care and
oversight of the Ury estate now devolved
upon Robert. Early the following year,
however, he started for London. He
petitioned the King for the redress of
certain grievances suffered by Friends,
and at the same time he presented an
address of acknowledgment drawn up by
the General Meeting of Aberdeen for
the Royal Declaration of Indulgence.
During his reign of three years, James,
himself a Catholic, had done all in his
power to force his own religion upon the
country, and had succeeded in alienating
the sympathies of all those who had

Photo. E. H. Lawton, Aberdeen.

MAUSOLEUM OF THE BARCLAYS, AT URY, NEAR STONEHAVEN.

supported him on his accession. The
bulk of the nation now refused to acknow-
ledge this Royal Declaration of Indulgence ; it granted religious toleration
to Catholics and Nonconformists alike,
and was considered a further menace to
Protestantism, besides being an attempt
on the part of the King to assert absolute
power.   Robert Barclay took no part in
"Vindi-   politics.   He wrote "I considered it not
cation." "my business to make a judgment of
"these things."   He   welcomed   the
Declaration of Indulgence as a step
towards the universal liberty of conscience which he, with others of his age,
in different sects, conceived as the only
solution of the problem of religious feud.

"Apol-   " This   forcing   of   men's   consciences,"
ogy,"
XIV., § 4. wrote Robert Barclay, " is contrary to sound
reason, and the very laws of nature.   For
man's understanding cannot be forced by all
the bodily sufferings another man can inflict
upon him, especially in matters spiritual. . .

By that course indeed men may be made hypocrites, but can never be made Christians ; " and hypocrisy, he adds, is " the worst of evils in matters of religion."

Barclay's last visit to London was an eventful one. He left Ury in March, 1688, and stayed the whole summer in London " visiting and serving his friends " to the utmost of his power." He placed his eldest son at Court during these months. He was an attractive boy and was much made of there. Meanwhile the King pursued his reckless policy, disregarding all warnings. On April 27th he issued his second Declaration of Indulgence, and in May ordered that this should be read on two successive Sundays in all churches throughout the Kingdom. The seven Bishops who protested against the King's action were arrested and confined in the Tower. The sympathy of practically the whole nation was with the Bishops ; Church-

men and Nonconformists forgot their
old quarrel in the presence of a common
danger. James endeavoured to win
over popular feeling to his side by
reference to the religious persecution
which the Church had sanctioned. He
said the Bishops were responsible for the
death of innocent men. This they denied.
Robert Barclay gained admittance to the
Tower, and had an interview with the
Bishops, setting before them facts, within
his own personal knowledge, of Friends
who died in prison, when confined by
Episcopal orders. But he said there was
no intention on the part of Friends to
publish these facts, or in any way to
strengthen the hands of the King against
them. The Bishops were brought to trial
and acquitted amid immense national
enthusiasm, and the same day a secret
message was despatched to William
of Orange inviting him to come over
and free the country from the tyranny of

James. The national distrust of James
had reached its height, and the birth
of a Prince at Whitehall had confirmed
the fear of a Catholic succession. His
last interview with James II. took place
at Whitehall, where, Robert the younger
tells us, his father stood long with the
King at one of the windows, discussing
the troublous state of affairs. James
had erected a weather-cock on one end of
the banqueting hall, which he could
watch from his private apartments, and
so tell whether the wind was Protestant
or Papist. He remarked to Robert
Barclay that the wind was now favour-
able for the coming of the Prince of
Orange. Robert said that it was hard
that no expedient could be found for
satisfying the people, and the King
declared that he would do anything rather
than part with the doctrine of liberty of
conscience. Whatever mistakes James
had made, Robert Barclay never doubted

the sincerity of his motives.   He wrote :

"Vindica-
tion."   " To do him right, I never found reason
to doubt his sincerity in the matter of liberty
of conscience. . . I must own, nor will I
decline to avow, that I love King James, that
I wish him well, that I have been and am
sensibly touched with a feeling of his mis-
fortunes, and that I can not excuse myself
from the duty of praying for him that God
may bless him and sanctify this affliction to
him.   And if so be His will to take from him
an earthly crown, He may prepare his heart
and direct his steps so that he may obtain
through mercy an heavenly one, which all
good Christians judge most preferable."

Robert Barclay sent his son back to
Ury in the autumn, after William of
Orange had landed in England. He
himself stayed in London till December,
when, after the flight of the King, he
returned home.

The two years which followed were
spent quietly at Ury, "enjoying him-

6

self," his son tells us " in visiting and "being visited by his friends and neigh- "bours." There is a passage in the " Apology " which gives us a clue to its author's tastes and pastimes. He wrote :

"Apol-
ogy,"
XV., § 9.   " That man should be always in the same intentiveness of mind, we do not plead, knowing how impossible it is, so long as we are clothed with this tabernacle of clay . . . [There] are . . . innocent divert- isements which may sufficiently serve for relaxation of the mind, such as for friends to visit one another ; to hear or read history ; to speak soberly of the present or past transactions ; to follow after gardening ; to use geometrical and mathematical experi- ments, and such other things of this nature."

There was great scope for gardening in the beautiful grounds at Ury.

The storms which had raged round Quakerism were now lulled to a large extent. But Robert Barclay was still singled out for fierce attack. His person and goods could no longer be touched, but he still came under the lash of slander. This did not surprise, nor greatly trouble him. But at the desire of his friends, he wrote a " Vindication," in which he answered the charges made against him.

The following letter was written to Sir David Carnegie, one of his friends, the year before his death and shows that his mind was busy with active schemes of some kind.

" Ury,

" Frind,   " 17th of 1st Mo. 1689.

" I am so indisposed I could not come to Drumlithie, and hope my man will come so timously to thee as to prevent thy trouble of coming from home. I have here sent thee my raw project which thou may see, it being the first and only coppy I have to receave the amendments of thy more mature judgment, which, when thou has perused and corrected, send to Johnston, that he may transmitt to Oldbair what thou and he sees meet, that at least will let those of Angus know what is our design. I shall expect coppy back on the next week, and the weather being tollerable iff in health, upon advertisement will meet thee when thou will appoint. This would be done as I said next week, that I may communicate what may be proper to some in Aberdeen.

" Mind my respects to thy Lady, who am thy assured frind,   " ROBERT BARCLAY.
" To Sir David Carnegie."[1]

There is only one other allusion to ill health in the course of Robert Barclay's life.   His son wrote :

" [As] if he had had a view of the shortness of his time in this world, he posted through all the affairs of life he thought incumbent upon him ; spending and bestowing his service, and for the benefit of all he could be helpful to."

In the year 1690 he was struck down with fever after returning from a meet-

[1] Seventh Report of Hist. MSS. Commission, Appendix, p. 724.

ing at Aberdeen. His illness was short
and painful, but suffering did not disturb
his peace of mind. These were his last
recorded words :

" Memoirs
of the Rise
. . of
the . .
Quakers
in the
North of
Scotland "
p. 448.
" Remember my love to Friends in Cum-
berland, at Swarthmore, and *to dear George*[1]
and to all the faithful every where. . .
God is good still : and though I am under a
great weight of sickness and weakness as to
my body, yet *my peace flows*. And this
I know, that whatever exercises may be
permitted to come upon me, they shall tend
to God's glory, and my salvation : and in
that I rest."

On October 3rd, 1690, Robert Barclay,
then in his forty-second year, ended
his work on earth. He was buried beside
his father.

A mausoleum was erected over the
Barclay vault, and to this is added a
modern structure, built by Alexander
Baird, who purchased the Ury Estate in

[1] Swarthmoor was the home of George Fox.

1854, when the last Barclay of Ury had
died. The old house was pulled down,
and no trace of this now remains, except
in the memories of the oldest inhabitants
of the district, who speak with a degree
of awe of its destruction, and of the
blasting asunder of the huge blocks of
stone with which it was built. But the
country has undergone few changes since
Robert Barclay lived and worked there.
There is more timber in Ury Glen, and
more building in the neighbourhood of
Stonehaven, which town is partly visible
to the traveller who takes his stand
at the Houff to-day and lets his eye
travel over the surrounding country.
One or two old farm buildings, black
belts of pines, golden stretches of gorse
and, to the east, the sea are what his
eye rests upon. It is a place of great
peace and stillness. Ury Glen, where
the old house stood, is richly wooded,
though the surrounding country is bleak

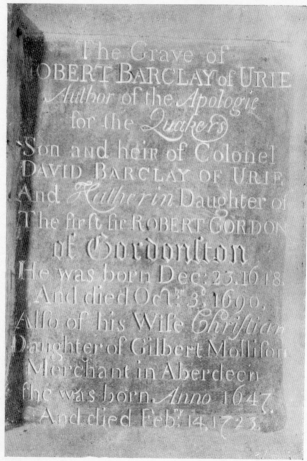

The Grave of
ROBERT BARCLAY of URIE
Author of the *Apologie*
for the *Quakers*
Son and heir of Colonel
DAVID BARCLAY OF URIE,
And *Katherin* Daughter of
The first Sir ROBERT GORDON
of Gordonston
He was born Dec: 23. 1648.
And died Oct.ʳ 3, 1690,
Also of his Wife *Christian*
Daughter of Gilbert Mollison
Merchant in Aberdeen
She was born *Anno* 1647.
And died Feb.ʳ 14. 1723.

TABLET IN THE MAUSOLEUM.

and bare. Here, as in his childhood,
Robert Barclay's home was situated in
a gentler spot than the surroundings
promised. At Gordonstown there was
always shelter and quiet when the winds
swept the plain that lies between the
Grampians and the sea. In these
surroundings took shape the character of
a man striking for its gentleness and power
of love. In an age that was harsh and
austere in many of its aspects, he was
able to show the beauty of family life, the
loveliness of Christ's law, and to reflect
very clearly the gladness which is promised
to His disciples. " I have never known
him in any peevish, angry, brittle, or
disordered temper," wrote one of his
friends of Robert Barclay; " I can say I
have parted with a most entire friend
and counsellor." His death left a great
gap in the fighting ranks of the new
Society, for his warfare on its behalf had
been very powerful. He had conquered

down the evil in himself, and so was able to meet and subdue it in others.

Christian Barclay survived her husband by thirty-two years. She was well fitted to be mistress of a large household ; her wise and loving rule did much to beautify the family life. George Fox wrote to her after her husband's death : " Cast thy care upon the Lord . . . who hath the breath and souls of all in His eternal, infinite hand. . . . Thou and thy family may rejoice that thou hadst such an offering to offer up unto the Lord."

CHAPTER VI

TRUTH TRIUMPHANT

AFTER his death, Robert Barclay's works were collected and published under the title "Truth Triumphant through the Spiritual Warfare, and Christian Labours and Writings of that Able and Faithful Servant of Jesus Christ, Robert Barclay." He took up the defence of his cause from every possible point. Quakers were accused of belittling the Scriptures, so he prepared an elaborate Catechism, dealing with doctrinal points raised by the Quakers. The answers were all given in the words of Scripture, and, as Robert Barclay said, Christ Himself was chief speaker.

A dispute arose among the Quakers

themselves as to the amount of authority which should be exercised in the Church of Christ. Some maintained that true Christian liberty was inconsistent with human restraint of any kind : Fox, the founder of the Society, upheld the belief that order was an essential part of liberty, and that those who were strong in the spirit must lead their weaker brethren. Robert Barclay faced this question of authority in a pamphlet usually known by the title of "The Anarchy of the Ranters." In it he vindicates Quakers from "those that accuse them of con-"fusion and disorder on the one hand, "and from such as calumniate them with "tyranny and imposition on the other." But the " Apology " which of late years has always been published in a separate volume, includes all that is greatest in his message, and most beautiful in his literary expression. In it the aim he set before himself was to give the world a clear statement of "the harmony of the truth we profess."[1]

He starts from the fundamental truth that "the height of all happiness is placed in the true knowledge of God." He shows that the testimony of the Spirit is that alone by which this knowledge is revealed, and that this knowledge is open to all, quoting what was known John i. 9. as the Quaker text "That was the true "light which lighteth every man that "cometh into the world." He shows further that the only way to attain to the knowledge of God is "to stand in His "presence, hear His voice, and observe the "motions of His Holy Spirit."

"Apol-
ogy."
XI., § 10. "He that cometh to learn of a master, if he expects to hear his master, and be instructed by him, must not continually be speaking of the matter to be taught, and never be quiet, otherwise, how shall his

[1] In this work Robert Barclay follows the order of propositions treated in the Westminster Confession.

master have time to instruct him? Yea,
though the scholar were never so earnest
to learn the science, yet would the master
have reason to reprove him, as untoward
and indocile, if he would always be meddling
of himself, and still speaking, and not wait
in silence patiently to hear his master in-
structing and teaching him."

Robert Barclay, in common with all the
followers of Fox, held that this waiting
upon God was not dependent upon time
or place.   But, he said,

"Apol-
oly."
XI., § 3.   " To meet together we think necessary for
the people of God ; because, so long as we
are clothed with this outward tabernacle,
there is a necessity to the entertaining of a
joint and visible fellowship, and bearing of
an outward testimony for God, and seeing
the faces of one another, that we concur with
our persons, as well as spirits."

In speaking of a Quaker Meeting,
he says :

"Apol-
ogy."
XI., § 17.

" As many candles lighted, and put in one place, do greatly augment the light, and make it more to shine forth, so when many are gathered together into the same life, there is more of the glory of God, and his power appears, to the refreshment of each individual; for that he partakes not only of the light and life raised in himself, but in all the rest. And therefore Christ hath particularly promised a blessing to such as assemble together in His name, seeing he will be in the midst of them."

And again :

"Apol-
ogy."
XI., § 7.

" So watching in a holy dependence upon the Lord, and meeting together not only outwardly in one place, but thus inwardly in one Spirit, and in one Name of Jesus, which is his power and virtue, they come thereby to enjoy and feel the arisings of this life, which, as it prevails in each particular, becomes as a flood of refreshment, and overspreads the whole meeting. . . And when any are, through the breaking forth of this power, constrained to utter a sentence

of exhortation or praise, or to breathe to
the Lord in prayer, then all are sensible of
it ; for the same life in them answers to
it, as in water face answereth to face. . .
Such is the evident certainty of that divine
strength that is communicated by thus meeting together, and waiting in silence upon
God, that sometimes when one hath come in,
that hath been unwatchful and wandering
in his mind, or suddenly out of the hurry of
outward business, . . so soon as he retires
himself inwardly, this power being in a good
measure raised in the whole meeting, will
suddenly lay hold upon his spirit, and won-
derfully help to raise up the good in him,
and beget him into the sense of the same
power."

This communication of divine strength
"Apol-   was to Robert Barclay a thing as certain
ogy."
II., § 16.   as the shining of the sun at noon-day.
He himself was " one that can speak from
"Apol-   " a certain experience, and not by mere
ogy."
XI., § 6.   " hearsay, of this wonderful and glorious
" dispensation." The belief in the im-

mediate revelation of God's spirit is the keystone of Robert Barclay's work on which all else depends ; it is the central point of the Quaker doctrine, because it is "That which all professors of Chris-"tianity, of what kind so-ever, are forced "ultimately to recur unto. . . the only "most true, certain, and unmoveable "foundation of all Christian faith."

"Apol-oly." II., § 16.

The power exercised by the early Friends, was due wholly to the fact that theirs was a religion of personal experience.

"Apol-ogy." XI., § 9.

"It must be," Robert Barclay says, " rather by a sensible experience, than by arguments, that men can be convinced of this thing, seeing it is not enough to believe it, if they come not also to enjoy and possess it."

The only preparation for the ministry which the early Friends desired was in a life lived in close dependence on God, and in the hallowing of every daily duty.

" Apol-
ogy,"
X., § 7.

To the question " How cometh a man to
"be a minister, pastor, or teacher, in the
"church of Christ ? " they had one em-
phatic answer, " By the inward power
"and virtue of the Spirit of God."   They
distrusted scholarship when it was re-
regarded as the necessary attribute of
a minister.   School Divinity Robert
Barclay regarded as " a monster," a
source of " endless janglings."

" Apol-
ogy,"
X., § 21.

" The volumes that have been written
about it, a man in his whole age could
scarcely read, though he lived to be very
old ; and when he has read them all, he has
but wrought himself a great deal more vexa-
tion and trouble of spirit than he had before."

Logic and philosophy, as taught in his
day he considered

" Apol-
ogy,"
X., § 20.

" the way to make a thing a great deal
darker than clearer. . . .   If ye would
make a man a fool to purpose that is not very
wise, do but teach him logic and philosophy ;

and whereas before he might have been fit for something, he shall then be fit for nothing, but to speak nonsense ; for these notions will so swim in his head, that they will make him extremely busy about nothing."

He does not condemn book learning as wrong in itself ; nor despise reason, "that noble and excellent faculty of the mind," nor fail to admit that "many things may contribute to further a work, which yet are not the main thing that makes the work go on."

"Apol-
ogy,"
II., § 14.
"Apol-
ogy,"
II., § 4.

It is only where "airy head-knowledge" comes to be regarded as a substitute for the "saving heart-knowledge," or as a cloak to conceal its absence that he condemns it.

"Apol-
ogy,"
X., § 23.

"What shall I then say," he wrote, "to you, who are lovers of learning, and admirers of knowledge ? Was not I also a lover and admirer of it, who also sought after it, according to my age and capacity ?"

He himself had given up all hope

of scholastic distinction in the sphere
naturally opening out before him, for,
having pursued knowledge with the
passion of a scholarly nature, he had,
as he tells us, laid down his wisdom
and learning " to learn of Jesus," and
then found himself called to receive
back all that he had yielded up, and to
use every talent and power with which
he was endowed, in the service of a
small suffering community, and in the
wider service of truth.

"Apol-
oly,"
VI., § 24.

The latter half of the " Apology "
deals with the special practices of Friends,
which Robert Barclay held to be the
logical outcome of their central belief. He
shows that as the baptism of the Spirit
may be received by all at all times, no
outward baptism is needed. As the
" true and spiritual supper of the Lord "
is that " which men come to partake of,
" by hearing the voice of Christ, and
" opening the door of their hearts, and so

"Apol-
ogy,"
XIII., § 3.

"letting him in," it is not the outward
Communion by which the "hungry and
fainting soul" is refreshed. He gives
his reasons for believing that Christ's
commands to baptise, and to observe the
Holy Communion, were no more bind-
ing with regard to external usage, than
His command to "wash one another's
feet," and hence, not finding the observ-
ance of the Sacraments "to be obligatory
upon us," Friends had discontinued
their use. To Robert Barclay all religious ceremonies were at best only
"types and shadows" of the substance,
which obscure the truth they are meant
to reveal, and become a source of controversy and bitterness. For those
"types and shadows" Episcopalians,
Presbyterians and Anabaptists were at
that moment "buffeting one another with
the scripture," ... " contending for this
"outward observation, and for the other
"outward observation, seeking Christ in

"Apol-
ogy,"
XIII., § 8.

"Apol-
ogy,"
II., § 13.
"Apol-
ogy,"
VI., § 24.

"this and the other external thing ... while
"in the meantime Christ lies crucified and
"slain, and is daily resisted and gainsayed
"in his appearance in their hearts."

"Truth
Trium-
phant,"
III.,
p. 524.

As for war, he says, " How men can
"love their enemies, and yet kill and
"destroy them, is more than I can reach."

Friends believed that a Christian should

"Truth
Trium-
phant,
III.,
p. 525.

not take an oath "for where the
"government of Christ prevails, and men
"speak truth, there all must confess,
"there is no need of oaths."

Much of Robert Barclay's work bears
the mark of his time. Violent and
abusive language in religious controversy
was, in the seventeenth century, the
rule and not the exception, and though
compared with contemporary pamphlets
his writings are strikingly free from
bitterness and railing, they do not
wholly escape criticism on this point.
He wrote for an age of greater leisure
than our own. He tells us more than

once in the " Apology " that he " studies brevity," but this fact may at times escape the notice of " the patient and unprejudiced reader." Much of the theological controversy which occupies the early propositions is now a thing of the past, and to-day many who believe fully in the central point of his teaching have set on one side, as non-essential, some of the details on which he lays stress, and feel that the list of " innocent divertisements " may even include such things as " to pipe, fiddle and sing," which he held to be very dangerous. To some extent the " Apology " has suffered from its admirers. During the eighteenth century it was accepted as the creed of the Society of Friends to the whole of which all members must subscribe. This extreme view produced a natural reaction, for no theological treatise can satisfy everyone, and nothing could have been less in accord with the spirit of Robert

Barclay's teaching, than that his personal opinions should be imposed upon succeeding generations. His strength lies in his belief that the ultimate appeal must be to the Divine spark in each man, and that there alone can he find his own gospel. Coupled with this is that other belief that as the Divine light, from which all human sparks emanate, is one and indivisible, so there must be unity in its ultimate manifestation, however much this may be disguised for a time by the imperfections of the human vessel. It had been no new gospel which transformed his life, only a fresh revelation of the old glad tidings, "The Lord is nigh to all them that call upon him." It was this which enabled the early Friends, "Apology." amid suffering and persecution, "to XI., § 13. testify of that joy" which they experienced.

To those who find themselves strangers to these revelations Robert Barclay says:

"Apol-
ogy."
II., § 16.
"Let such know that the secret light which shines in the heart and reproves unrighteousness, is the small beginning of the revelation of God's spirit. . . . Wait then . . . in the small revelation of that pure light . . . and as thou becomest fitted for it, thou shalt receive more and more."

EXTRACT FROM ROBERT BARCLAY'S TRACT ON "PEACE."

"Wherein the true cause of the present war[1] is discovered, and the right remedy and means for a firm and settled peace is proposed."

---

[1] Between Louis XIV. and the Dutch.

AN EPISTLE OF LOVE AND FRIENDLY ADVICE.[1]

To the Ambassadors *and* Deputies *of the* Christian Princes *and* States *met at* Nimeguen, *to Consult the Peace of* Christendom, R. B. *a Servant of* Jesus Christ, *and hearty Well-wisher to the* Christian World, *Wishes Increase of Grace and Peace, and the Spirit of sound Judgment, with Hearts inclined and willing to Receive and Obey the Counsel of* GOD.

Let it not seem strange unto you, who are Men Chosen and Authorized by the Great Monarchs and States of *Europe* to find out a speedy Remedy for the present great Trouble (under which many of her Inhabitants do groan) as such, whose Wisdom and Prudence, and Abilities have so recommended them to the World, as to be judged fit for so Great and Difficult a Work, To be

[1] A copy of this letter, in Latin, and a volume containing the "Apology," was delivered on February 24th, 1678, to each of the ambassadors and deputies who met to sign the Treaty of Nymwegen.

Addressed unto by one, who by the World
may be esteemed Weak and Foolish ; whose
Advice is not Ushered unto you by the Commission of any of the Princes of this World,
nor Seconded by the Recommendation of
any Earthly State : For since your Work
is that which concerns all Christians ; why
may not every Christian, who feels himself
stir'd up of the Lord thereunto, contribute
therein ? And if they have Place to be heard
in this Affair, who come in the Name of
Kings and *Princes ;* let it not seem heavy
unto you to hear him, that comes in the
Name of the *Lord Jesus Christ.* . .

Know then, *My Friends*, that many and
often times my Soul has been deeply bowed
down under the Weighty Sense of the present
State of Christendom ; and in secret before
the Lord I have mourned, and bitterly
lamented because thereof. And as I was
Crossing the Sea, and being the last Summer
in *Holland*, and some Parts of *Germany*,
the Burthen thereof fell often upon me, and
it several Times came before me to write
unto you, what I then saw and felt from

God of these Things, while I was in those Parts. But I Waited, and was not willing to be Hasty ; and now being returned to my own Country, and at my own Home, I chearfully accept the fit Season, which the Lord has put in my Hand, and called me to therein. . . .

The *Chief Ground*, *Cause* and *Root* then of all this Misery among all those called *Christians*, is, Because they are only such in Name, and not in Nature, having only a Form and Profession of Christianity in Shew and Words, but are still Strangers, yea, and Enemies to the Life and Virtue of it ; owning *God* and *Christ* in Words, but denying them in Works ; And therefore the Lord Jesus Christ will not own them as his Children, nor Disciples. For while they say, they are his *Followers ;* while they Preach and exalt his Precepts ; while they Extol his Life, Patience and Meekness, his Self-denying, perfect Resignation and Obedience to the Will of his Father ; yet themselves are out of it : And so bring Shame and Reproach to that Honourable Name, which they assume

to themselves in the Face of the Nations,
and give an Occasion for Infidels (*Turks,
Jews* and *Atheists*) to Profane and Blaspheme
the Holy Name of *Jesus*. Is it not so? . . .
While upon every slender Praetext, such as
*Their own small Discontents, or That they
judge, the present Peace they have with their
Neighbour, cannot suit with their Grandeur
and Worldly Glory*, They *sheath their Swords
in one another's Bowels; Ruine, waste and
destroy whole Countreys; Expose to the
greatest Misery many Thousand Families;
Make Thousands of Widows, and Ten
Thousands of Orphans;* . . . And all this
while they pretend to be *Followers of the
Lamb-like Jesus;* who *came not to destroy
Men's Lives, but to save them;* The Song of
whose Appearance to the World was, *Glory to
God in the Highest, and Good Will and Peace to
all Men*; Not to Kill, Murther and Destroy
Men; not to hire and force poor Men to
run upon and murther one another, meerly
to satisfy the Lust and Ambition of Great
Men; they being often-times Ignorant of
the Ground of the Quarrel, and not having

the least Occasion of Evil Will or Prejudice against those their *Fellow-Christians*, whom they thus Kill; amongst whom not one of a Thousand perhaps ever saw one another before. Yea, is it not so, that there is only a *Name*, and *nothing of the True Nature* of Christians especially manifest in the *Clergy*, who pretend not only to be *Professors*, but *Preachers*, *Promoters* and *Exhorters* of others to Christianity, who for the most Part are the greatest Promoters and Advancers of those Wars; and by whom upon all such Occasions the Name of God and Jesus Christ is most horribly abused, prophaned and blasphemed, While they dare *Pray to God, and Thank him for the Destruction of their Brethren Christians*, and that for and against, according to the Changeable Wills of their several Princes : Yea, so that some will join in their Prayers with and for the *Prosperity* of such, as their *Profession* obliges them to believe to be *Heretical* and *Antichristian*; and for the Destruction of those, whom the same *Profession* acknowledges to be *Good* and *Orthodox Christians*. Thus the

French, both *Papists* and *Protestants, Join in their Prayers and Rejoice for the Destruction of the* Spanish Papists *and* Dutch Protestants. *The like may be said of the* Danish, Swedish *and* German Protestants, *as respectively concerned in this Matter.* Yea, which is yet more strange, if either Constraint or Interest do engage any Prince or State to change his Party, while the same War and Cause remains; then will the Clergy presently accommodate their Prayers to the Case, *In Praying for Prosperity to those, to whom instantly before they wished Ruine;* and so on the contrary; As in this present War, in the Case of the *Bishop of Munster* is manifest. Was there ever, or can there be any more horrible Profanation of the Holy and Pure Name of *God*, especially to be done by those, who pretend to be Worshippers of the true God, and Disciples of *Jesus Christ?* This not only Equals, but far Exceeds the Wickedness of the *Heathens;* For they only Prayed such Gods to their Assistance, as they fancied allowed their Ambition, and accounted their Warring a

Virtue ; whom they judged Changeable like themselves, and subject to such Quarrels among themselves, as they that are their Worshippers ; But for those to be found in these Things, who believe, there is but *One only God*, and have, or at least profess to have such Notions of his Justice, Equity and Mercy, and of the Certainty of his Punishing the Transgressors of his Law, is so horrible and abominable, as cannot sufficiently be neither said, nor written.

The *Ground* then of all this is the Want of *True Christianity*, because the Nature of it is not begotten, nor brought forth in those called *Christians ;* as therefore they bear not the Image, nor bring not forth the Fruits of it. For albeit they have the Name, yet the Nature they are Strangers to ; The Lamb's Nature is not in them, but the Doggish Nature, the Wolfish Nature, that will still be quarrelling and destroying ; the Cunning, Serpentine, Subtle Nature, and the Proud, Ambitious Luciferian Nature, that sets Princes and States a work to contrive and foment Wars, and engages People to

fight together, some for Ambition and vain
Glory ; and some for Covetousness and Hope
of Gain : And the same Cause doth move
the Clergy to concur with their Share in
Making their Prayers Turn and Twine ;
and so all are here out from the State of
True Christianity. And as they keep the
Name of being Christians ; so also upon the
same Pretext each will pretend to be for
Peace, while their Fruits manifestly declare
the Contrary. And how . . . doth
Experience daily discover this Deceit ! For
how is Peace brought about ? Is it not,
when the Weaker is forced to give way to the
Stronger, without Respect to the Equity of
the Cause ? Is it not just so, as among the
wild and devouring Beasts ? Who when they
Fight together, the Weaker is forced to give
way to the Stronger and so desist, until
another Occasion offer ? So who are found
Weakest, who are least capable to hold out,
they must bear the Inconveniency ; and he
gets the most Advantage, however frivolous,
yea, unjust his Pretence be, who is most able
to vindicate his Claim, and preserve it not by

Equity, but Force of Arms; So that the
Peace-Contrivers Rule is not the Equity of
the Cause, but the Power of the Parties. Is
not this known and manifest in many, if
not most of the Pacifications, that have been
made in Christendom? . . .

Try and Examine your selves therefore
seriously in the Sight of God, whether you
be Led, Acted and Influenced in your present
Negotiation by the Wisdom of this World
. . . or by the *Heavenly* and *Pure
Wisdom of God.* . . If the Warring Part
be removed out of you . . . then are
you fit to consult and bring about the Peace
of Christendom, . . . Whereof, and of all
those that Profess the Name of Christ I am,

A True Friend, and

Hearty Well wisher,

ROBERT BARCLAY.

*This came upon me from the Lord to
write unto You at* Ury, *in my Native Country of* Scotland, *the Second of the Month
called* November, 1677.

Letter from Lady Gordon to David Barclay.

"Gordonstown, July 17th, 1663.

Dear Son,

"I received yours from London the 13th approximo; was exceedingly glad to hear that you were well, for I did long much to hear from you. Both your little boys have had the pox very favourably. David was not sick at all with them, but John had three days of fever, but it hath done him much good, for he is now very lusty and begins to find his tongue. . . . I bless God for the resolution to fetch your son, although your Brother would not send him to you to the Rhine, yet I cannot believe that he will keep him against your will. You shall do well to walk wisely to get your son with the consent of his Uncle, but if he will not, then you were better want his kindness than buy it with the loss of your son. Let not therefore the hope of worldly gain persuade you, but remember who hath said I will never leave not forsake you, which certainly He will make good to all that walk in His commandments. . . . I desire you to see your little ones bred in the ways of God, and I shall pray the Lord to continue you to them, and that they may be comforts to you. This is the prayer of your affectionate Mother to serve you.

"Lucé Gordon."

BOOKS USED.

"Truth Triumphant," in three volumes. Printed 1718.

The "Apology," a reprint by William Irwin, 1850.

"Genealogical Account of the Barclays of Urie," written by the son of the Apologist, 1740.

"A Short Account of the Life and Writings of Robert Barclay," by David Barclay, of Walthamstow, 1802.

"Robert Barclay, the Apologist of Quakerism," by B. Rhodes.

Articles in the *Theological Review*, 1874 and 1875, entitled :

   (I.) "The Great Laird of Ury."

   (II.) "The Marrow of Barclay," by Alexander Gordon.